A Servant's Guide
From
A Servant's Heart
Ministry From A-Z

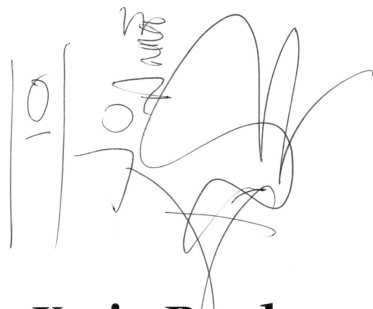

Kevin Bond

Printed in the United States of America

ISBN here

This book is dedicated to all who endeavor to serve God in a
real way. It is also dedicated to all who have been hurt in the
process, yet continue to serve God. I pray that this manual will be
beneficial to the body of Christ and to society at large.

Written by: Kevin Bond
Edited by: Adrian Nesbitt
Cover Photos: Ernest Washington and Amadi Phillips

CONTENTS

My Gratitude

I FIRST THANK GOD FOR my newfound passion as a writer. He has blessed me to be very successful in music over the years, and I trust that he will help me to fulfill all that he has purposed for me in this endeavor as well. I have been writing for many years, but until now had never completed any of my works. I'm grateful to present to you a book that I hope will bless ministry leaders for years to come; a book that I have not only written, but also lived.

TO MY FAMILY:

I would like to thank my wife, Toni, for her 13 years of continued love and support. I am aware that many couples long for a relationship such as ours--one that's rooted in a love for God and each other; centered on our mutual fulfillment. Honey, this is the beginning of the next phase we prayed about some years ago. I Love You! I am also grateful to our children--Tayler, Alex, Kiara, and Phillip. I pray that Daddy is making you proud to carry the name Bond. You truly are making us proud! Your development and growth is paramount to your mother and me. We love you!

TO MY PARENTS, PASTOR ALEX T. BOND, JR. AND ESTELLA BOND:

This has been an incredible journey. Dad, you've been healed to be a witness to the healing powers of God. I mirror you in so many ways that it's scary at times! To this day, you remain as my greatest hero and life teacher! Mom, you showed me what a godly wife and mother is through your love for Christ and your family. It's because of the example you set that I was able to find my queen! Congratulations to you both for 50 years of love and matrimony! WOW!!! And I remarried you!!!

TO ALL MY MENTORS AND TEACHERS WHO PLAYED A PART IN MY DEVELOPMENT:

I THANK YOU! If I attempted to list you all, I would need another book. But know this; I'm much taller today because I stand on your shoulders. You are truly some of God's greatest giants. Thank you for pushing me forward and for pulling me aside for correction, when necessary. Thanks also for speaking life into me when I needed it most. Had you not done so, I have no idea where I would be now. I'm blessed to have you all as great mentors.

TO ALL OF THOSE WHO HAVE SUPPORTED MY MINISTRY THROUGH THE YEARS:

I'm truly grateful for every CD you've purchased, every email you've sent, every prayer you've prayed, and every dollar you've sown into my ministry. Today, I am equally grateful that you've sown into this new ministry that God has bestowed upon me. Thank you! Thank you! Thank you!

TO MY EDITOR, ADRIAN NESBITT:

Thank you for helping to make this dream a reality. You're truly a Levite that God has anointed for more than music! I pray that this experience urges you to explore even more of what God has planned for you. LaTonya, thanks for sharing Adrian with the world for the creation of this kingdom work.

FOREWORD

OVER THE YEARS I have consistently encountered two types of people in ministry--the prepared and the unprepared. Those who have been prepared for ministry inevitably are able to minister effectively as a result of their years of preparation. But for every one who has been prepared, there's another who's not been adequately prepared, and is, therefore, far less effective than they might otherwise have been.

I have always thought that it would be tremendously useful if a ministry guide existed that would point out the essential characteristics vital to one's success in serving; a simple guidebook offering practical insight and inspiration for a life of extraordinary service.

Certainly, such a book would be tailor-made for those who sincerely want to serve but are clueless as to where to start. And, it would be no less helpful to those who are presently serving and aiming to sharpen their skill and minister even more effectively. Many point to the Bible as that resource--and it is! But I'm sure all will agree that we can greatly benefit from sound teaching that illuminates the Bible's profound truths and spurs us on to act on them.

This was the catalyst for the book you now hold. While seasoned leaders may already know what are the essential personal characteristics needed for ministry and service, those humbly seeking an opportunity to serve may not. Thus, there is a great need for such instruction. Kevin Bond has provided just that.

His concise, empowering book is aptly entitled, "**A Servant's Guide from a Servant's Heart: Ministry from A to Z.**" I pray that you will not only read it, but also apply each and every quality he's so richly detailed here.

Ronn Elmore, Psy.d; Author-Speaker

OPENING

THE WORD IS FULFILLING itself in that the harvest is truly ripe but the laborers are few. The truth is we need more laborers in the vineyard. But we need them to be properly equipped for service. Otherwise, they will be ineffective.

With all of that in mind, I have prepared a book that details what to look for, as well as ways to know if ministry and service is for you. I've detailed the necessary characteristics for anyone seeking to serve in a tangible way.

This resource is not for those just wanting to be seen. It's not for those seeking a position for which they want glory or credit. Neither is this manual for anyone who wants to matriculate through the ranks of ministry for their services rendered. Rather, it's for those who are sincere and passionate about both the things of God and the people of God. It's for those who feel that God is leading them into a life or season of service for him. It's for those who feel that God is greater than all and that his programs should also reflect that. Finally, it's for the ones who would like to give back to God the talents and abilities given them.

The songwriter wrote, "What shall I render unto God for all his blessings." He answered his own question by stating, "All I can render is my body and soul. That's all I can render. That's all I can give." If you identify with these words, this book is for you.

As you read this book, I pray that you are not turned away from service. Instead, it is my prayer that it motivates you to become more than you are now, building upon the characteristics and skills you currently possess. The truth of the matter is that many who are serving now were not fully prepared when they started either. So there's no need to feel inferior or surmise that you must grow to some astronomical level before you can begin to serve. <u>Effective service is a process, and only those who have been processed can serve effectively.</u> God has been processing you all along for this moment. Remember, he always equips those whom he calls, and he always prepares those for the assignment at hand. But we must endeavor to keep our tools sharpened and ready for use.

So prepare to take self-examination as you sharpen your skills for service through this manual, which I've simply entitled, "**A Servant's Guide from a Servant's Heart: Ministry from A to Z.**"

What Is A Servant?
Written by: Kevin Bond

*A servant is someone who is **able** to lead as well as follow;*
*One who is **bold**, **confident**, and **dependable.***
*A servant is someone who can **esteem** others as well as*
*himself; **Fearless** in the face of opposition,*
*and **godly** towards all.*
A servant is someone who walks in
humility** and **integrity;
***Just** in all his dealings, **kind**, **loving** and **meek**.*
*A servant is someone who is **nameless,***
***open-minded and patient**;*
***Quiet** in the face of adversity and*
***resilient** in the face of defeat.*
*A servant is someone who is **stable,***
thoughtful, and unselfish; Valiant,
*but **willing** to fight when necessary.*
*A servant is someone willing to **x-ray** every circumstance;*
*One who is **yielded** to the cause of Christ;*
***Zealous** for the will and purposes of God!*

What Is A Servant? I Am A Servant!

ABILITY

Able: having the power, skill, means,
or opportunity to do something

THE ONE WHO IS **able** leads my ministry guide. Much like a beautiful field of green grass, ministry is very attractive from afar. When looking across a field, one only sees what appear to be perfectly formed blades of grass, seemingly void of imperfection. Only upon closer examination do perception and reality part ways.

Masks and deception abound in ministry. The one who is **not able** often creates the unreal perception that he is **well able** when he is really **unable**. By speaking well of his great skill and avoiding any admission of weaknesses, the inadequate ministry leader has learned the art of talking a good game. The problem is, however, that he has no **ability** to produce results. He does possess an undeniable desire and willingness to lead, but that's not enough. The effective ministry leader must be **able**! He must be **able** to lead, able to take responsibility, **able** to change, and **able** to accept changes.

When Jesus chose his disciples, he sought for those who were **able** to further his ministry. Knowing the life of his ministry would be short, Jesus pursued individuals who were **able** to quickly grab his vision and carry it forward after he had left them. Far too often we choose people with great ideas but have no real **ability** to implement them. They are always boasting about what they've done in the past, but they are yielding no fruit in the present. God is in need of servants who are not just great talkers, but also great doers; those that not only avail themselves when called, but come with gear in hand, prepared and **able** to get the job done.

Jesus' method of choosing his co-laborers gives us an excellent model. What did he do? He visited each of them, taking note of both their skills and their **ability** to work effectively within their given professions. Although they faltered in their service at times, they never faltered in their **ability** to do the job.

Now, I have a few simple questions to ask you: Are you flexible; **able** to change, mold, and adapt to different challenges, tasks, and personalities? Are you **able** to respect authority and follow instructions? Are you **able** to show up for the assignment and **able** to complete the assignment? If yes, then you are now ready to go to the next step in this ministry guide.

Now say with me, *"I am **able** to do that which God has called me to do!"*

MY SERVANTHOOD NOTES

_____

_____

_____

_____

_____

_____

_____

_____

_____

_____

_____

_____

_____

_____

BOLDNESS

Boldness: showing an ability to take risks;
confident and courageous

BOLDNESS CAN BE DEFINED as fearlessness in the face of impending danger. It is one of the most important elements of a leader's arsenal. The **bold** servant is confident enough to stand strong in situations that would send others cowering in fear. **Boldness** is the driving force that guides us over the rough terrain we're often forced to travel. I say *over* because **boldness** doesn't back down. **Boldness** neither quivers nor throws in the towel. **Boldness** says, "I'm aware of the risks, but I was born to take risks, and will gladly do so for the cause of Christ."

Boldness is related to an inner confidence that says that an idea is doable or that a goal is attainable. When others would accept defeat, the **bold** servant says, "There must be a way because God inspired the idea, and his word tells me that I'm more than a conqueror." **Boldness** says, "I won't stop until the desire is fulfilled, the task completed, and I have received the seal of approval from heaven."

Boldness is what led a youthful lad named David to fight a giant named Goliath. While all others around him were terrified of the giant, David showed why he would soon become Israel's leader. **Boldness** led David into the face of danger; then to his ultimate triumph over the giant. It wasn't David's bow that defeated Goliath. It was his **boldness**!

Consider Joshua, who displayed great **boldness** after taking over for the deceased Moses. Without Joshua's **boldness**, God's people would never have reached the Promised Land. Wow! One man's **boldness** affected an entire nation!

A leader's **boldness** can lead him through doors that cowards can only dream of entering. Many opportunities are forfeited on account of leadership's cowardice!

Are you **bold** enough to pursue all that God has placed within you? Are you **bold** enough to take it by force? Are you **bold** enough to take a stand and not waver? I believe you are!

Say with me now: *I'm as **bold** as a lion! I will remain fearless in the face of danger and all obstacles! I can do all things through Christ who strengthens me!*

MY SERVANTHOOD NOTES

_____

_____

_____

_____

_____

_____

_____

_____

_____

_____

_____

_____

_____

_____

_____

Confidence

Confidence: the quality or state of being certain,
convinced, and sure

CONFIDENCE IS THAT INNER feeling of trust in one's correctness and competence. The **confident** leader boasts of an absolute certainty of his ability. Even when others around him are doubtful, his **confidence** ultimately rests in his knowledge that God is with him. Friends, there is no greater **confidence** than that which comes from knowing that God is with us.

Confidence is what has driven Bill Gates, Donald Trump, Ted Turner and other great entrepreneurs to become successful and amass great wealth. I'm certain that they all had skeptics who doubted their plans, but these men exercised an inner **confidence** that pushed them past all discouragement into great reward. One of my favorite verses says, "Therefore, don't throw away your **confidence**, which has a great reward" *(Hebrews 10:35)*. When leaders are **confident**, rewards follow!

Confidence is the *but* in the sentence of a negative

report; it's the *why not* to the person who seemingly has the right answer; it's the *go ahead* to the one with the gut feeling; it's the *what if* to the one who knows that there is another option!

At many stages in my life I've moved ahead in **confidence**, despite the reservations of others. And each time, the dividends from moving ahead in **confidence** were greater than even the **confidence** it took to make the decision.

Confidence is what drove a little-known biblical character named Caleb to tell the leadership to stop speaking negatively and move forward. Caleb's **confidence** gave him the courage to speak up, despite the fact that his stance was vastly unpopular. You too must be willing to take such a stand if called upon to serve.

By now you know what comes next. Repeat with me:

I am **confident** *in the things of God. I will walk in all that God has purposed for my life, and I will build* **confidence** *in those which God has placed around me.*

MY SERVANTHOOD NOTES

_____

_____

_____

_____

_____

_____

_____

_____

_____

_____

_____

_____

_____

_____

DEPENDABILITY

Dependability: trustworthy and reliable:
capable of being depended on

SUPPOSE YOU REQUESTED PEOPLE to sign up to serve dinner to the elderly. Let's say you had 60 volunteers, but only 15 showed. That means that only those 15 proved to be **dependable**. The other 45 of them showed that they were not **dependable**.

Just because you stand in a garage doesn't mean you'll become a car! In much the same way, a statement of **dependability** doesn't deem it to be so.

Dependability is not known by a mere verbal statement of intention or commitment. Rather, it can only be proven by one's consistent adherence to his verbal commitments. **Dependability, then, implies that there is something we must become as well as a quality we must possess.** If a leader consistently fails to honor his commitments, he lacks **dependability** and loses the trust of his people.

To be **dependable** means that not only can our pastors count on us, but those whom we serve can count on us as well.

Dependability is such a critical attribute because it implies trustworthiness. And at the core of any relationship, there must be trust. When a leader loses the trust of his followers, he has failed as a leader.

Apostle Paul had a serious problem with John-Mark early on in his ministry because John-Mark was not **dependable**. While he should have stood confident during Paul's tough times, John-Mark left Paul out ministering and went back home where things were much safer. Paul learned something early on to which many of us could attest. He learned that only those who are **dependable** will stand with us during hard times. Later on, Paul did send for John-Mark, but only after he had proven himself **dependable**.

Like Paul, I have experienced similar situations with those I thought were in my inner circle. There have been times when I've partnered with or hired the ones I thought were most qualified for the job, only to find out later that they were not **dependable**.

Too often in ministry, the people with the greatest talent are the ones on whom ministry can't **depend**. Great talent plus little **dependability** amounts to overwhelming frustration for those whom we serve. In fact, the smart ministry will accept lesser talent for greater **dependability**!

Are you **dependable**? Can God count on you? We have all been faced with that question at some time or another. Choose today whom you'll serve and commit to him completely!

Now if you agree with this affirmation, say with me, "God can **depend** on me! I am **dependable**!"

MY SERVANTHOOD NOTES

_____

_____

_____

_____

_____

_____

_____

_____

_____

_____

_____

_____

_____

_____

Esteem

Esteem: the regard in which one is held;
worth; value.

WHAT DO YOU THINK about yourself? Do you feel good about yourself? Do you value where God has you now? Do you feel valuable to the kingdom? How do you feel about others? Do you feel comfortable with the fact that there are others who are as gifted as you are? Can you **esteem** others? These simple questions lie at the base of the word **esteem**.

Good **self-esteem** is essential for ministry service. When we possess healthy **self-esteem**, we are able to lead others to places they may never have thought of going. Good **self-esteem** empowers us to be able to speak into people's lives and push them into their ultimate destinies. Moreover, when ministry leaders feel good about themselves, followers sense it. They see the confidence and poise, and want to follow.

Without good **self-esteem**, ministry leaders are

powerless. And almost inevitably, their ministries will reflect that powerlessness. When ministry leaders lack healthy **esteem**, they often operate from a place of intimidation. As a result, everybody suffers! On the contrary, a leader with good **self-esteem** will attract others with good **self-esteem**. Consequently, he will build an organization with good **self-esteem**.

Not only must we possess healthy **self-esteem**, we must also be able to **esteem** others. Ministry often presents the challenge of having to **esteem**, or build up, others even when it's difficult to do so.

I recently stumbled across a picture of an eye. I can hear you now asking, "What's so special about an eye?" But what was unique about it was that the eye was made of diamonds, rubies, and emeralds. I believe that the artist was telling us that we should see as God sees. Through his eyes, God sees us all as precious stones.

We should see the value in others as the diamonds after which we fawn. We should see the depth in others' character as the fine rubies; and we should see the preciousness of the hearts of all with whom we come in contact as the emeralds.

As God sees greatness in others, so should we recognize the greatness in others. As we acknowledge the greatness in others, we affect their attitudes and inspire them to do more and be better.

Say with me:

I feel good about me! I can help you feel good about

you! And because God made us both in his image and likeness, I can see us as he does!

People of worth and value, **esteem** yourself and others greatly.

MY SERVANTHOOD NOTES

_____

_____

_____

_____

_____

_____

_____

_____

_____

_____

_____

_____

_____

_____

_____

FAITHFULNESS

Faithful: steadfast in affection or allegiance; loyal

I RECALL A POPULAR SONG that we used to sing years ago. The lyrics read, "Be ye steadfast, unmovable, always abounding in the work of the Lord." As a young man, I saw that song as one which spoke primarily about the rewards of labor. Now that I'm older, however, I realize that the song was not only speaking about reward, but about **faithfulness**. **Faithfulness**, allegiance to a cause or entity, is a critically necessary characteristic of ministry leaders.

Unfortunately, **faithfulness** is widely lacking in our modern society. In a day when the love of money has contaminated the purity of ministry, many leaders have even abandoned their **faithfulness** to God. **Faithfulness** to materialistic possessions has usurped the priority of God. People are fickle and are easily swayed by the opinions of others. They often lose focus quickly, committing in word; never in deed. But in order to be effective in ministry, we must display **faithfulness** toward the things of God. One writer said that "if you don't stand for something, you will fall for anything." Just as **unfaithfulness** in a spouse leads to infidelity, and **unfaithfulness** in the workplace leads to unemployment, **unfaithfulness** to God causes us to forfeit the blessings of relationship with him.

Conversely, many of us are **faithful** to a fault. Our **faithfulness** is misplaced. Misplaced **faithfulness** makes us easy targets for those who prey on the **faithful,** but undiscerning, individual. We must not only be **faithful,** but also able to judge to whom we should be **faithful**. If we're unable to discern where our **faithfulness** should lie, we become vulnerable to the attack of the predator ministry. The predator ministry consists of individuals who have made it there life's mission to **faithfully** prey on the **faithful**. So I urge you to use discernment in choosing the ministry or individual to which you can be **faithful.** And remember always that God can see what we don't see. While we're looking at the outer appearance of a situation, he's constantly checking the heart of the matter. Remain **faithful** to him and trust his leading at all times.

*Lord, I vow to remain **faithful** to you, and I thank you for being **faithful** to me. Help me now to be **faithful** to all whom you've commissioned me to serve.*

MY SERVANTHOOD NOTES

_____

_____

_____

_____

_____

_____

_____

_____

_____

_____

_____

_____

_____

_____

_____

Gentleness

*Gentle: free from harshness, sternness,
or violence*

THE INTERESTING THING ABOUT this definition is that in defining what **gentleness** *is*, it addresses what **gentleness** *isn't*. To be **gentle** is to *not* be harsh, stern, or violent. **Gentleness** speaks of kindness, peace and friendliness. <u>The leader who deals successfully with others must master **gentleness**</u>!

As ministry leaders, we will sometimes encounter hostile people and situations. There are those who feel like their way is the only way and that all other individuals only exist to deny them the things they want most! It's at that place that the one with a **gentle** spirit can influence change. The **gentle-spirited** leader can ease an otherwise hostile situation by the way he speaks and handles himself under intense pressure. It's an awesome gift to be able to diffuse a chaotic situation by the **gentleness** of our words and demeanor.

I've been on both sides of the fence, and I appreciate the **gentle** spirit that God has now placed within me. I am no longer the troublemaker I used to be. Thank God for change! LOL!!!

Gentleness gives us the ability to regulate the temperature in any place or situation. Proverbs 15:1 says, "A **gentle** answer turns away wrath, but a harsh word stirs up anger." Imagine us having the power to change the temperature of our relationships just by our presence or speech. When we allow **gentleness** to be a part of our character, we graciously assume that power to affect change.

In 2 Samuel 22:36, David boasts of the **gentleness** of the Lord. He writes, "Thou hast also given me the shield of Thy salvation: and Thy **gentleness** hath made me great." Leaders, our **gentleness** is even powerful to propel others into greatness! And because **gentleness** is a fruit of the Spirit, we can all possess it when God's Spirit dwells within us.

Say with me: *I am a **gentle** spirit. God created me to be a **gentle** spirit. I shall not let circumstances control me, but I shall control my circumstances.*

MY SERVANTHOOD NOTES

_____

_____

_____

_____

_____

_____

_____

_____

_____

_____

_____

_____

_____

HUMILITY

Humble: not proud or haughty;
not arrogant or assertive

WITH ALL OF THE power and influence that's associated with leadership, there is perhaps no greater potential hazard to a celebrated leader than the emergence of pride and arrogance. The truly successful leader, however, must reject pride and walk in **humility**. Maintaining **humility** is a serious challenge for great leaders. Unfortunately, many have lost that struggle to remain **humble**.

Often times it is not the service that makes us proud and haughty, but the titles. It's important to note, however, that titles are not the essence of who we are. Our titles in ministry are only applicable at the ministry. Although we are titled at church, we are only husband, wife, mom, and dad at home. For many leaders, titles have caused self-inflated opinions that only cause harm to the body of Christ.

When God places it in man's heart to promote us to

titled positions of service, we cannot allow ourselves to become proud and arrogant. After all, God is the one who exalts us!

Psalm 75:4-7 speaks adamantly against arrogance:

4 To the arrogant I say, 'Boast no more,'
and to the wicked, 'Do not lift up your horns.

5 Do not lift your horns against heaven;
do not speak with outstretched neck.'

6 No one from the east or the west
or from the desert can exalt a man.

7 But it is God who judges:
He brings one down, he exalts another.

Many in ministry claim that they're not arrogant--just confident. But as I explained earlier, confidence is being certain of one's abilities; not looking down on another's abilities. Unlike confidence, pride and arrogance always offend others. If Christ could **humble** himself to the point of leaving a throne in heaven to die for our faults, certainly we should have no problem **humbling** ourselves to serve those same people for whom he also died.

Here's my definition of **humility**: "The ability to respect and honor others who possess less than we do." It is being able to make ourselves low even when we're in a high seat.

David is perhaps the best model of **humility**. You may recall that although he was anointed king, Saul was still the reigning king. David could have become arrogant and demand that Saul be killed. Or he could have even killed Saul himself. But he refused to touch the set man on the throne. He **humbled** himself in order to honor Saul, knowing that he already was Saul's replacement.

How would you have handled that situation? Could you have honored the one who was sitting in your newly appointed seat without ever telling him in the heat of the moment that he had lost his title? Could you have **humbled** yourself in the presence of someone who refused to **humble** himself before God?

Before we proclaim this one, we should repent for all the times we have failed at this point. And for me, it's been a lot!

*Father, forgive us for refusing to **humble** ourselves. Thank you for giving us another chance to master this principle today. We vow to remain **humble** no matter how high you take us and no matter how much honor you bestow upon us. We will cherish those whom you've called us to serve, and we now stand **humbly** at your feet to do so. Amen.*

MY SERVANTHOOD NOTES

_____

_____

_____

_____

_____

_____

_____

_____

_____

_____

_____

_____

_____

INTEGRITY

Integrity: firm adherence to a code of especially moral or artistic values; incorruptibility

THE VERY ESSENCE OF **integrity** is the existence of an undeniable agreement between what we say and what we do! When there is a conflict between our speech and our actions, the result will always be corruption. As its definition implies, **integrity** connotes incorruptibility. Only to the extent that we practice what we preach will we be able to build ministry that commands the respect of saints and sinners alike. Leaders must walk in **integrity**!

Many in leadership have corrupted the system by exhibiting behavior contrary to the messages they have spoken. But we must remember that people do what they see more than they do what they hear. As my Mom used to say, "They can't hear what you're saying for watching what you're doing." If there is a single greatest deterrent to sinners accepting Christ, I believe it's the dichotomy that they too often witness between our everyday lives and our Sunday morning ministry performance.

Paul said it best when he encouraged the people to "follow me as I follow Christ." That statement is **integrity** personified. Paul was putting himself on the line by stating that "if I'm not following Christ, then don't you follow me." I love the fact that he was unwilling to compromise the lives of his people by following any example other than Jesus Christ.

It's been said that **integrity** is doing the right thing even when no one is looking. It's who we are when we are alone. Now that's a scary thought for some of us.

Before we can lead effectively, we must master our own soul's desires. As Paul (my favorite biblical character) stated, we must "bring our bodies under subjection." We must know our weaknesses as well as our strengths. We must not pray for God to deliver us from evil, yet hang around the very things that tempt us to sin. God has always and will continue to use imperfect people to do his perfect work, but we should not use our weaknesses as scapegoats for our own disobedience.

It's important to note that **integrity** is partner to discipline. The two go hand in hand. The former involves the training to build moral character, while the latter is the adherence to all that we have been trained to do.

Jesus possessed this quality, and so must we. It is essential for us if we intend to be light in an otherwise dark world. We can't just be light to those already in the light, but we must allow God to use our light to deliver the world from its darkness. Our actions will speak louder than any words we could ever articulate.

Father, help us now to practice all that you've taught us. Thank you for calling us to kingdom work. We will walk in **integrity** *and bring our bodies under subjection to your will and purposes.*

MY SERVANTHOOD NOTES

_____

_____

_____

_____

_____

_____

_____

_____

_____

_____

_____

_____

_____

_____

JUSTICE

*Just: acting or being in conformity with what is
morally upright or good*

WHEN I WAS A child, my father would always say to me, "If you don't stand for something, son, you'll fall for anything." That statement has driven me to take many unpopular stands over the years. But the one thing I have always tried to do is stand for what I believe is right! The **just** leader does precisely that. He stands on the side of truth, never conforming to the schemes and plans of immoral people, even when they have more influence than he has.

Standing for what's right is not always easy. In fact, it is particularly difficult when standing against those who have more authority than we have. I'm not suggesting that we should fight openly with our adversaries. We're never correct to disrespect authority in public forums. The Bible even says that we should agree with our adversaries quickly. But we should never waver from truth. At the end of the day, we are to stand for what's right in the eyes of God.

Ministry attracts all kinds of people. And along with a diversity of people comes a diversity of opinions. Inevitably, we will be faced with making choices between what is right and what is popular. Or, as I've heard it said, we'll have to decide between good ideas and God ideas.

All good ideas are not God ideas. And more often than not, the crowd is wrong. Remember the story of Paul's imprisonment in Acts 27 when the crowd urged the keepers to set sail in the face of boisterous winds? Although Paul cautioned that they should not set sail, the crowd went against his advice. That decision forced them into shipwreck. Only God's presence and Paul's right standing kept them alive. Nevertheless, the penalty for a bad decision was the loss of the ship, loss of all of their belongings, shattered courage, and shaken faith.

Justice can never be measured by what the majority says is right. Instead, the **just** man always stands for what is right and good, despite the dissent of the crowd. The **just** shall life by faith!

*Lord, lead us toward the path that's right and good. Help us to be **just** in all of our dealings. Let us be the earthly example of your will and purpose.*

MY SERVANTHOOD NOTES

_____

_____

_____

_____

_____

_____

_____

_____

_____

_____

_____

_____

_____

_____

_____

_____

KINDNESS

Kind: affectionate; loving

THE LEADER WHO IS **kind** has a warm and tender spirit. He is easily approachable and very caring toward the needs of others. **Kindness** is a crucial attribute of a godly leader. Without **kindness**, a leader will suffer greatly in his ability to win others to the faith. Moreover, unpleasant interpersonal relationships with others will ultimately undermine a leader's entire ministry. Paul even encourages us to be **kindly** affectionate toward one another *(Romans 12:10)*.

Being **kind** means that we're willing to care for others. It means that we're not afraid to openly display our emotions. This is important in an age when we are made to think that if we show our emotions or feelings, we are weak. But more often than not, if we think it's a weakness, God sees it as strength!

Jesus, weeping at the tomb of Lazarus, openly displayed his emotional attachment, or **kindness**, to his friend *(John 11:35)*. At a moment when many of us would have tried to hold it all together publicly, Jesus showed us that it's okay to care. It's okay to weep. And it's okay to openly love others.

Remember the lone leper who returned to thank Jesus upon receiving his healing? The other nine chose not to show their appreciation to Jesus. And this one leper could've easily followed suit. Instead, he chose to return and show **kindness** to Jesus. By doing so, his action has been canonized in the scriptures so that we all may see that **kindness** has great reward.

The ministry road leads us across the paths of many wounded souls. These individuals often need our extension of **kindness** towards them. We must take time to not only speak a **kind** word, but also show them that we care through our acts of **kindness**. People trust us by what we do, not by what we say.

Our young people are seeking **kind** ministers who care for them and are willing to touch them, if necessary, to save them. I recall many instances as I was ministering to people, there came a point when no more words were needed. Instead, a touch or act of **kindness** was necessary. So much so that I had to stop speaking and touch, sometimes embracing, the one to whom I was ministering. It was at that point that the healing and full range of ministry began. Never be afraid to go beyond words into deeds! More than a word or song, a **kind** touch goes a long way toward reaching the lost. **Kindness** touches the heart!

*Father, we now ask that you release **kindness** in your people again--the **kindness** that was exhibited in your son, Jesus. We vow today to follow the example he set for us.*

MY SERVANTHOOD NOTES

_____

_____

_____

_____

_____

_____

_____

_____

_____

_____

_____

_____

_____

_____

LOVE

Loving: to hold dear; cherish

A T THE HEART OF any ministry, there *must* be one indispensable quality--the quality of **love**. Apart from it, no ministry can operate according to God's standards. Unfortunately, many ministry leaders are performing the duties of ministry, but lack the **love** that makes ministry truly effective.

The apostle Paul speaks to us clearly regarding the priority of **love.** He reminds us that without **love**, all of our work is worthless. He writes that faith, hope, and **love** are all key factors. But the greatest of them is **love** *(1 Corinthians 13).*

Jesus notes that we prove to the world that we are his, indeed, if we **love** one another *(John 13:35).* Notice that he doesn't say that if we wear the custom suit, dress, or shoes. Nor does he say if we live in the best neighborhood, drive the best car, or have a wealthy 401k. He says that the full proof of our discipleship is whether or not we have **love** for one another.

It's important to note that the **love** we show should extend not just to believers, but to sinners as well. The effective ministry leader must be able to **love** the sinner and hate the sin. He must be able to **love** the sinner *through* the snare of sin. Whether through adultery, drug addiction, homosexuality, or some other sexual immorality, the leader must **love** just as Christ **loved** him while he himself was in sin. He must never forget that he was the recipient of that same **love** before being rescued from the bondage of sin.

He must also **love** the people to whom he ministers. And he must **love** them more than he **loves** the position or title that he holds. Too many leaders would rather minister apart from **love**, choosing rather to prance around on stage in awe of their own titles. But titles only describe the office. They don't define the individual. It's impossible to minister effectively if we are more enamored with our titles than we are in **love** with God's people. If we don't **love** people, we are unprepared for ministry.

Paul states that **love** covers a multitude of sins. If that's true, then the **love** we have for one another will cover us all *through* our weaknesses. If we operate with a **loving** heart, we'll resist the urge to talk about one another; we'll resist the urge to tear one another down; and we'll resist the urge to become judgmental. Instead, we'll encourage each other to be all that God called us to be.

Paul also says that **love** never fails. In other words, **love** never becomes ineffective. It always works! Though some gifts will fade away, **love** will always endure. And in our fast paced world with new devices and technologies evolving everyday, it's good to know that there remains one constant--LOVE.

When we **love** each other with godly **love**, our issues with each other diminish. Indeed, **love** has much power! Incidentally, over 2000 years ago, **love** *moved* the Father to action. John 3:16 says that God so **loved** the world that he *gave* his only son. How powerful is **love** that it could move us to action? If you're reading this book today, you've been moved to action--the action of service. Just be certain that you mix **love** with the service. Remember Paul's admonition-- without **love** our service is worthless!

*Father, I **love** you. I also **love** my brothers and sisters here on earth. I now choose to follow your example to **love** for the rest of my days.*

MY SERVANTHOOD NOTES

_____

_____

_____

_____

_____

_____

_____

_____

_____

_____

_____

_____

_____

_____

MEEKNESS

Meek: enduring injury with patience and without resentment or retaliation

HOW DO YOU FEEL when people speak negatively of you? Can you handle people disagreeing with your leadership? What is your response when folk rebel against you and coerce others to follow in rebellion? Do these scenarios cause you to seethe in anger and contemplate revenge? If not, you're in good shape. But if these scenarios bother you, perhaps you should ask God for a dose of **meekness.**

When we think of **meekness**, most of us think of passivity, weakness, and unassertiveness. Being *meek* is generally translated as being *weak*. **Meekness**, however, is actually the opposite of this popular misconception. **Meekness** involves strength. **Meekness** entails remaining tempered even after we've been injured, without retaliating. What an incredible challenge--even for the super-saint! But it's a necessary characteristic of an effective ministry leader.

   Meekness is imperative because ministry is not always easy. Actually, it's rarely easy at all. Ministry is often bloody, grueling, tiring, and draining. Many people only see the exterior side of ministry and are drawn to what appears to be power, glamour, and a life of ease. The reality, however, is that ministry is often abusive and injurious.

   Throughout all of scripture, there is no greater example of **meekness** than that which was displayed by Christ. He endured tremendous pain and suffering without ever striking back at those inflicting it. His **meekness** was, in fact, born out of love. Likewise, if we are going to truly cultivate **meekness**, it must be born out of our love for God and others. Christ's example offers us great encouragement to walk in Paul's instruction to "endure hardness as a good soldier" *(2 Timothy 2:3).*

   To develop **meekness** is to develop a thick skin that can endure the pain that ministry sometimes brings. But we can rejoice knowing that God has made some promises to the **meek**. He says that they shall eat and be satisfied; they shall be guided in judgment and taught his ways; they shall inherit the earth; they shall delight in the abundance of peace; and one of my favorites, they shall be beautified with salvation *(Psalms 25:9, 37:11, 149:4).* There's a special place carved out just for the **meek**. At that place, God blesses the **meek** because of all that they willingly endure for his sake. That's good news!!!

Decree with me:

*Lord, I choose to walk in **meekness** and allow you to avenge my adversaries. I offer my scars back to you to mend them. Heal me as I journey back to those whom you've sent me to serve as minister. And I ask that you would forgive them; for they knew not what they were doing.*

MY SERVANTHOOD NOTES

NAMELESSNESS

Nameless: not known by name; anonymous

I LOVE THIS ONE. IT separates the serious from the self-seeking. To remain **nameless** is to do the work but not receive the credit. It is to be willing to serve without recognition; to give all but never get our name called. That's a tough thing considering that we all like to be recognized occasionally. But leaders must be characterized by a willingness to operate in **namelessness**.

I'm finding that at this hour the Holy Spirit is flowing so greatly in our worship services that there is no time for commercials. There was once a time when we would pause, call names, and take bows for the work we had done. But that was yesterday. Today, there's no room for flesh to be on parade. The truth is, there was never room; we just made room. But now more than ever, God is looking for soldiers who can get the spoils so that all can enjoy the victory; soldiers who have come to the realization that if one wins, everybody wins; soldiers who are in it for the good of the team; soldiers who are not self-centered, but God-centered. I say soldiers, not individuals; not stars; not divas, or prima donnas!

Paul's epitaph of Jesus sums this one up for us all. He said that Christ made of himself no reputation, and took upon him the form of a servant, and was made in the likeness of men: And being found in fashion as a man, he humbled himself, and became obedient unto death, even the death of the cross *(Philippians 2:7-8)*.

All that Jesus did was for the kingdom at large--not for himself. His decision to die for us was not for a feather in his cap or a hero's welcome. Can you serve without seeking recognition from man? Can you lay it all on the line for God and trust his reward?

Paul rounded out his memoirs of Jesus by saying that because of all he endured, God highly exalted Jesus, giving him a name above all other names.

As you ponder this point, I trust that the Christ in you is saying, "Yes, Lord, I'm willing to remain **nameless** and allow you to exalt me in due season."

*God, I thank you for showing me this principle clearly. Through your power, I know I can remain **nameless** for the advancement of the kingdom. Your name is the only name that needs to be called, and I gladly proclaim the name of Christ the risen King.*

MY SERVANTHOOD NOTES

_____

_____

_____

_____

_____

_____

_____

_____

_____

_____

_____

_____

_____

_____

Open-mindedness

Open-minded: receptive to arguments or ideas

J ESUS' DECISION TO CHOOSE Peter and Thomas as his disciples was a clear representation of his **open-mindedness** as a leader. Between Peter's many challenges and Thomas' doubting, Jesus definitely had his hands full. But Jesus looked beyond their foibles and chose them as part of his inner circle anyway. No doubt, Peter and Thomas' friends were appalled at such a decision, but Jesus' **open-mindedness** allowed him to go against popular opinion and see greatness in two less than stellar characters.

As ministry leaders we are faced with opposition and rebuttal on a regular basis. How we receive such arguments is directly related to our **open-mindedness**. How we respond to change reveals to those serving with us whether or not we are **open-minded** leaders or close-minded fools. The extent to which we are willing to learn new things and explore new methods determines how much we are willing to grow as leaders.

There's nothing worse than a leader who acts as if he knows it all; one who is close-minded to others' ideas, yet expects everyone to champion his. The day we stop learning is the day we die. Perhaps not a physical death, but we are certain to at least die intellectually and interpersonally. The leader who alienates others will soon find himself alone in a desolate place. Consequently, in times of critical decisions, he will be without counsel to aid him. *No Man is an Island* is more than a song. God purposely created us to co-exist interdependently.

As leaders we must always trust God, knowing that he sends people to help implement the vision he places inside of us. And while there can only be one head and one vision, God sends others to build upon that vision. Indeed, many of us are enjoying the fruits of harvests we didn't plant because we linked up with an **open-minded** leader.

Father, I ask that you keep my mind open to new things and new ideas. Help me to continue to grow. Please place people around me with the same passion for knowledge and growth. Help me remain open to hear from you, open to follow you, and open to serve you for the rest of my life.

MY SERVANTHOOD NOTES

_____

_____

_____

_____

_____

_____

_____

_____

_____

_____

_____

_____

_____

_____

_____

PATIENCE

*Patient: bearing pains or trials calmly or
without complaint*

WHILE WE ALL CAN define **patience**
in theory, few of us have been able to master
the practice of it. Servants must be **patient** people.
Ministry is not hurried, so it's imperative that we have
the capacity to wait and trust God to act on our behalf.
We must always remember that there are souls at stake;
therefore, we can never rush the processes of God at the
risk of losing those souls.

The children of Israel suffered the consequences of
their lack of **patience** thousands of years ago. They
couldn't handle the challenges of the desert, so they
started complaining. They didn't realize that before
making it to the Promised Land, they would have to first
venture through the desert process. Without **patience**,
their frustrations set in, delaying the manifestation of
God's promise to them.

I have had to exercise **patience** many times through

dry places in my life. It was in those places that I learned to trust God more. In the process, I developed the fruit of **patience**. Far too often we do just as the Israelites did--complain and murmur during challenging times. And worse, many of us die right in the heart of our wildernesses because we lack the **patience** to endure.

Patience is not the absence of pain, but the forbearance of it. It's not being bitter about a situation; it's trusting God to help us handle it. It's maintaining calmness and a peaceful spirit in the midst of our storms.

In ministry, God's timetable will rarely synchronize with ours. The vision we have for our ministry will not manifest until God is ready for its manifestation. That process of waiting on God requires **patience. Patience** is the capacity to accept or tolerate delay, trouble, or suffering without getting angry or upset. It's knowing that God controls everything above, around, and under our feet, no matter how much hell is breaking loose. It's complete reliance upon him in the midst of the problem. It's the ability to rest in the fact that's it's his assignment that we're carrying out. And he will bring it to pass only according to his schedule.

Patience is acquired over time, not overnight. It takes much prayer to learn to take our hands off of situations and trust God to handle them. Abraham and Sarah had to learn that the hard way. They tried to help God when he was seemingly taking too long to give them their promised child. What resulted was Ishmael, son of the bondwoman; not Isaac, the chosen seed. Whenever we get impatient and refuse to wait for God's timing, we run the risk of giving birth to an Ishmael. Ishmael represents bondage.

Let us not forget that while it seems that their plan succeeded with the birth of Ishmael, he and his mother were ultimately expelled from the household. That's because God is not in the substitution business. That which he promises, he's able to perform and bring to pass. Only when we choose to be **patient** can we enjoy the privilege of giving birth to Isaac, or God's blessed seed; the child of promise; the vision God alone can bring to pass.

Please learn this principle--it's a most important lesson: *God doesn't need our help. What he requires is our **patience**, mixed with faith and trust.*

Pray about the area where you've been impatient and ask now for forgiveness. God is trying to build something in and through your trial.

*Father, give us the **patience** of Job, who received a double portion of your blessings after his personal encounter with you. Give us **patience** to know that no matter how long it takes, we must take you on the journey while we wait. Give us **patience** that transcends time, season, and reason. Amen.*

MY SERVANTHOOD NOTES

_____

_____

_____

_____

_____

_____

_____

_____

_____

_____

_____

_____

_____

_____

_____

QUIETNESS

Quiet: marked by little or no motion or activity

"And that ye study to be **quiet**..." *(1 Thessalonians 4:11)*

MINISTRY SOMETIMES CALLS FOR **quietness**. In those moments we must, as Oswald Chambers writes, "do only the duty that lies nearest." We must do only our immediate assignment and do it without outside distractions.

I like watching television shows about the people who work behind the scenes. When I watch my favorite shows, it's obvious to me that a lot of work goes into their production. What's not obvious, however, is *who* does all of the hard work. In fact, I only get a glimpse of those individuals' names at the end of the show as the credits are rapidly scrolling down the screen.

That's what it means to be **quiet**--to function in ministry without all the fanfare or hoopla. Indeed, that's a tough task for leaders who can't function without a crowd and a bullhorn. These leaders tell others what they're working on long before they ever write a plan or chart a course of action. In recognition of their frenzied ways, the Bible calls these persons busybodies.

In contrast, the **quiet** servant can rally the troops and get the job done with few words and little wasted motion. He can mobilize a group of people without others ever knowing what's going on. But he can be equally effective while working alone. He possesses the confidence I spoke of earlier to do the work in **quiet** anonymity, and his work always yields great dividends. In fact, it is he-- not the noisemakers out front-- who is the true backbone of ministry. He is to the ministry what the blood is to the body; what the brain is to the head; and what the veins are to the heart. The Bible says that it is the parts of the body we can't see that deserve more honor (1 Corinthians 12:23). They are just as valuable, if not more valuable, than the parts that we do see.

To the **quiet**-spirited persons, I commend you. To those who desire to be like them, repeat these words:

*Lord, **quiet** my spirit that I may work with my hands as you command me to do; that I may speak only when necessary; and that I may be effective for you in the kingdom. Amen.*

MY SERVANTHOOD NOTES

_____

_____

_____

_____

_____

_____

_____

_____

_____

_____

_____

_____

_____

_____

Resilience

Resilient: tending to recover from or adjust easily to misfortune or change

HOW IS YOUR REFLEX-ABILITY? Do you adapt to change quickly? Are you able to bounce back when misfortune strikes? If you are a **resilient** leader, then all of your answers to these questions will be affirmative.

Before you begin to think that this point will disqualify you from your ministerial privilege, let me encourage you. God has built **resilience** within us all. **Resilience** is what allowed Moses to lead the children of Israel through the wilderness for 40 years. It sustained Joseph and Paul while locked in prison. And John the Revelator possessed so much **resilience** that he was able to write his vision while in exile on the isle of Patmos.

Resilient folk are often considered to be courageous and fearless because they allow nothing to stop them once they're focused on a goal. If you think back, you'll discover that **resilience** was the force behind many of your toughest victories.

Ministry demands **resilience**! It is next to impossible to function as a servant without it. I can recall many points in my life when my **resilience** was the only thing that sustained me during transitional points. Whether it was my release from a job or ministry assignment, or just waiting on God to bring a vision to pass, I had to remain **resilient** through each of these life-changing phases.

Change is inevitable, but if we possess **resilience** we'll never be caught off guard by change. The winds of life are constantly blowing, but the **resilient** possesses the rudder to steer through and over rough seas to smoother waters.

I can recall one time in particular when I was released from a job while putting the finishing touches on my first custom home. Yes, I was fired while preparing to move into my house--all within a two-week span. While this effort took a massive amount of faith, it also required a **resilient** mindset to not crack under intense pressure.

To anyone that may be dealing with a similar situation, I should also add that as a result of my **resilience**, my family moved into that home and my clientele tripled! It seems that God was testing me to see whether or not I would trust him and rely on all that he had placed within me. I'm proud to say that I believe I passed that test!

If you're still up to the challenge-- and I believe you are--say this with me:

I am **resilient***. Neither change nor misfortune can stop me. I can bounce back from all that comes my way because God made me to be* **resilient,** *just like he is!*

MY SERVANTHOOD NOTES

STABILITY

Stable: firmly established; fixed, steadfast; not changing or fluctuating; unvarying; permanent; enduring

STABILITY IS THE ABILITY to stand firm when all else around us is wavering. Do you follow the crowd? Or can you stand firmly alone? One of my favorite sayings is, "birds flock together, but eagles fly alone." The eagle is willing to take a stand when other birds are not. It flies a little higher than the others, positioning itself to better view its surroundings. Moreover, it's unwilling to compromise its position for the sake of having other birds fly along. The eagle survives the storm! As I think about it, I've never driven past a dead eagle. But I have driven past many other species of dead birds.

Like the eagle, a servant must be willing to take a stand even if it's a lonely one. He must be willing to soar above all others to get the best possible perspective on every situation. He must never fluctuate in the choices he makes or the path he takes. This is not in contrast to resilience, but in conjunction with it. The successful leader is not fickle, tossed aside by every wind. By contrast, the successful leader is a **stable** one.

During his three years of ministry, Jesus gave us a perfect example of **stability**. The Pharisees and Sadducees, his harshest critics, were always accusing him of blasphemy. Yet he never wavered. Instead, he valiantly endured and remained **stable,** even when ridiculed by the masses.

In one instance, the people wanted to stone him, but he stood steadfast in his doctrine and the teachings of his Father. And in an amazing act of boldness, he walked through the angry crowd and continued his ministry.

We're all familiar with the crucifixion--how Jesus could have come down from the cross, but endured the shame and ridicule of his adversaries. That single act of **stability** has become the most enduring and permanent example of the Christian faith. In fact, it's the reason why I'm able to write to you today!

If you're able to remain **stable** and hold your ground in the midst of this fickle society, God is seeking you. Too many people decide to serve, only to be swayed by people and pressure. But God is searching for those who will remain faithful as Christ did.

If that's you, then say with me:

*"Lord, **stabilize** me in all I do for you. Your foundation is solid and sure, and I choose to build my foundation in you."*

MY SERVANTHOOD NOTES

THANKFULNESS

Thankful: expressing gratitude and relief; conscious of benefit received

THANKFULNESS, OR GRATITUDE, IS one of the most important pieces in a servant's cache of essentials. The **thankful** servant is ever mindful of the grace he receives, and never exhibits condescension or indifference toward those he serves. By contrast, the leader who feels his ministry deserves him, or that he is "God's gift," often lacks any real sense of **thankfulness.**

Gratitude should permeate the hearts and minds of ministry leaders. Not only should we be **thankful** toward God, but we must never fail to recognize and acknowledge the greatness of those among us.

The scriptures are replete with commands that we assume a **thankful** posture as we live the Christian life. Psalm 100 even asserts that before we can offer up legitimate praise, we must first have an attitude of **thanks**. Our gratitude must be an attitude! Before we can offer praise in his courts, we must first enter his gates with **thanksgiving** in our hearts. **Thanksgiving** precedes praise. I'm almost certain that we can better strive to honor this principle in our service to God.

Paul, who persecuted many Christians before his conversion, was never negligent in his attitude of gratitude. In fact, in many of his writings, he used the phrase, "**thanks** be to God." Paul realized that had God not intervened in his life of persecution toward Christians, he would have missed his opportunity to be in relationship with God. After Paul's conversion, he never missed an opportunity to **thank** God for the gift of salvation, for his life, or for the love and support of the saints. <u>Like Paul, we must always be **thankful** to God and realize that our service *for him* is the gift that we offer back *to him* for all of his benefits *toward us.*</u>

Finally, the **thankful** ministry leader is aware of the fact that it is God who chose and ordained him for the position he now holds. He realizes that he does not need to try to impress man, because God is the one who grants promotion. Proverbs 18:16 declares, "A man's gift makes room for him and brings him before great men." The book of James follows suit and declares that every good and perfect gift comes down from the Father. Therefore, all gifts, abilities, and service opportunities point back to God. He's responsible for where we are and all that we have. Our responsibility is only to maintain a **thankful** attitude as we are blessed with such gifts.

Now recite these words with me:

*"Lord, I **thank** you for placing me where I am. I **thank** you for trusting me to lead your people, and I **thank** you for ordaining me before the foundations of the world to do this work."*

MY SERVANTHOOD NOTES

_____

_____

_____

_____

_____

_____

_____

_____

_____

_____

_____

_____

_____

_____

_____

UNSELFISHNESS

Unselfish: not selfish; generous

THE TRUE SERVANT LEADER must **not be selfish**, but generous towards those whom he serves. Whether through the impartation of knowledge and advice, or the offering of some other assistance, he must willingly share that which God has given him to build the kingdom, without withholding information that can benefit others.

As ministry leaders, we must be willing to build up others even if they are likely to get the greater position in the end. We should be so **unselfish** that we're actually working ourselves out of a job as a result of our **unselfishness**. We should be so busy passing down all God has given us that another will soon be able to occupy our present position. I like to say it this way: "Promotion only comes when you become overqualified at your present position." Our **unselfishness** should be driving us to deposit all that we have into those whom we serve. We must empower them to do all the work we do and more.

Are you **unselfish** enough to share with others all that you know so God can take you higher? Can you pour your all into others so that they can go to the next level? Can you do it namelessly? It is not uncommon for the ministry leader to help establish the success of his followers, only to have them forget all his labor of love when they have attained a higher position.

I'm sure you remember the story of Joseph. The butler forgot about Joseph when he was restored to his position. With one word he could have had Joseph restored as well. But that didn't happen-- at least not right away. Rather than become bitter and serve the remainder of his sentence in prison with malice in his heart, Joseph chose to trust God. What he did for the butler was a truly **unselfish** act, with no strings attached.

Unlike Joseph, many of us give to others with the expectation that we will get something in return. We give with the notion that all of our giving will be reciprocated. But we must guard against such a false notion. Although the Word does say that if we give, it will be given back to us, it doesn't say that we'll receive it *from* the person to whom we gave it. Likewise, the Word tells us that if we sow, we shall reap. But it doesn't say that we'll reap *where* we sowed. Never fret about helping and sowing into the lives of others, because the **unselfish** servant will always be blessed. God promised it!

Speak these words with me:

*Lord, less of me and more of thee. I choose to give all that I have to another for your sake and for the sake of the kingdom. I choose to live an **unselfish** lifestyle, trusting that as I give, you'll give back to me one hundredfold. I realize that as long as I focus on you, I'll see Christ in those whom I serve. And, Lord, as you served **unselfishly**, so now do I.*

MY SERVANTHOOD NOTES

_____

_____

_____

_____

_____

_____

_____

_____

_____

_____

_____

_____

_____

_____

_____

Valiance

Valiant: possessing or acting with bravery or boldness; courageous

A S I WAS WATCHING a Western once, I saw an advertisement for a bounty hunter which stated, "Only brave souls need apply." I wish that there were such an advertisement for ministry leadership. Ministry requires brave and courageous souls. It requires those who are not afraid to take the plunge. Ministry is not about passing or failing, but about serving effectively and **valiantly**.

To be **valiant** not only speaks of courage, but also of determination. O that there were more **valiant** servants with the determination of the apostles in the book of Acts. These apostles were so focused and determined that they would not let anything stop them from spreading the message of the Gospel. Even when the widows broached the apostles with their complaints, the apostles refused to stop devoting their time to the ministry. Instead, they appointed seven men to aid them in ministry. They were actually quantifying the need for servanthood.

Their endurance of all that they did to spread the Good News reveals the courage and determination they possessed. They were beaten, stoned, spat upon, imprisoned, and some even beheaded. Thank God we don't have to give our lives to serve him. Yet ministry service still requires **valiance**, courage, and determination.

Valiance was used to describe David when he was only a shepherd boy. David, in defense of his sheep, had the boldness to take on a lion and a bear. He was brave enough to stand against the giant, Goliath. And he was courageous enough to organize his mighty men and lead them to triumph over their enemies.

Like David, the servant leader must be **valiant** in his office. He must not be afraid of the lions and bears of ministry; the doubters who won't believe in his purpose; or the spectators who are standing by to see if he will fail or give up on God. But he must be **valiant** in the face of all those who speak against the thing about which he is most passionate.

Valiance will defeat the toughest foes every time. It is the will- power that is necessary to do the impossible. It is the heart of a warrior just before battle. It is the belief that no matter what, he can and will be victorious. God placed this trait within us before the foundations of the world. Now we must draw from it!

Let's recite together the words that God spoke to Joshua:

*"Be strong and of a good courage; be not afraid, neither be thou dismayed: for the Lord thy God is with thee whithersoever thou goest." I am **valiant** and determined to do all that God requires of me!*

MY SERVANTHOOD NOTES

WILLINGNESS

Willing: prompt to act or respond; ready

MINISTRY LEADERS MUST BE both **willing** and able. Ability without **willingness** is worthless. A **willing** vessel is what God is seeking today; someone who will give all for the sake of the kingdom; someone **willing** to do all that he can do for his brother or sister. A **willing** vessel will always offer to help in any situation. He never considers it an imposition to serve or help someone else. In fact, he will go out of his way to make others comfortable, happy, or satisfied. Although one's personal satisfaction is a difficult achievement, the **willing**-spirited leader will never stop trying.

I find these types of people rare and hard to come by. We often see the same people serving in churches, schools, and businesses. Some of us feel that it's actually a disservice to be called upon all the time; but not the **willing** vessel. He considers it an honor to give without expecting anything in return. In fact, the **willing** servant is often underpaid, under appreciated, and in many instances, taken for granted. Yet he is always ready whenever called upon. What would ministry be today without the **willing**? How far could the message go without a **willing**, ready soul to help carry it?

I now ask, "What is the motivation behind your service?" Is it simply your **willingness** to serve God, or is there some other motive or hidden agenda that will soon surface? I pray that it's a genuine love and care for God's people. As long as your motive is pure, nothing and no one will be able to break your **willingness** to serve.

*Lord, I thank you for your stellar example of service. Grant me now a pure motive and a **willingness** to serve your people; not only in the proud moments, but also the difficult ones.*

MY SERVANTHOOD NOTES

_____

_____

_____

_____

_____

_____

_____

_____

_____

_____

_____

_____

_____

_____

X-RAY

X-Ray: to examine, treat, or photograph
with X-rays

I PARTICULARLY LIKE THIS WORD because of all that its definition implies. One in ministry must be able to examine each situation and treat it as a separate occurrence. He must also be able to use word pictures to help others understand, or stand under, the authority and teachings of Jesus Christ.

One of the biggest challenges in ministry is to not stereotype or broad-brush those whom we serve. We have to make clear judgment calls with each situation. We must resist the inclination to group everyone into the same boat, even if situations are similar. A doctor treats hundreds of patients every year, but he maintains a chart that's unique to each of his patients. He must never confuse one with the other. Neither can he forget the treatment he prescribes to each patient.

In much the same way, a minister must keep clear, concise records of each of those to whom he ministers or gives counsel. He must also remember the treatment he uses to help each of his followers. If the leader doesn't keep up with this information, he could end up treating the same issue for many years without any results.

Sadly, that's what happens in many churches on a weekly basis. In an effort to help EVERYONE we rarely focus on ANYONE, and ultimately NO ONE benefits from ANY ONE of our solutions.

Medication is only useful if it is tailored for the needs of the one who is sick. It is similar to using a drug that is sold over the counter versus a prescribed drug. The prescription drug will hone in on the specific illness, while often times the counter drug will not. The counter drug may help for a brief time, but it won't solve the core problem. This is how true ministry works. It must be suitable to the growth and development of the whole man and not just a part.

This issue of **x-raying** a situation is akin to using discernment. A servant with a discerning spirit can see things others can't with the naked eye. He can see deep inside the heart of man. It's as if God has given him powers that he alone possesses. The discerning servant will be careful to ask the proper questions to get the proper answers. He will look beyond the surface at the core of the matter, seeing as God sees and hearing as God hears.

Through prayer and submission to God, all can have our discernment sharpened. It starts by taking heed to the voice of God. As we pay attention to the little things God says, we'll begin to hone in on the things others say as well. We'll also begin to see within the heart of man and develop a better understanding for many of the situations we encounter.

Remember, before any act of surgery goes forth, the doctor always calls for an **x-ray**. We too should **x-ray** individuals before suggesting a remedy for their problems. We must pray for the discernment necessary to visualize the things of God in the hearts of his people. We should never make a long-term decision with a short-term solution.

*Father, I thank you for the gift of discernment. I thank you for those reading the book today. They are seeking greater discernment as well. Lord, help us to discern your voice in all that we do. Help us to discern your will in the lives of your people. Lastly, grant us the ability to **x-ray** each and every situation, prescribing only the solutions that you speak to us. Amen.*

MY SERVANTHOOD NOTES

YIELDEDNESS

Yield: to give up possession, claim, or demand: as a) to give up (as one's breath) and so die b) to surrender or relinquish to the physical control of another: hand over possession of c) to submit (oneself) to another

A S WE NEAR THE end of this book, please pay close attention to the last two terms. This word, *yieldedness*, must be at the core of anything we do. We must give up our possession of everything we do for God.

The very first thing we must surrender is the claim on our lives. The Bible states that we were bought with a price. Therefore, we must glorify God in both body and spirit *(1 Corinthians 6:20)*. The servant who is unwilling to surrender to God is not a servant of God, but of himself. Either we serve God or we're serving ourselves. In many passages throughout scripture, God is referred to as a jealous God; therefore, only the **yielded** servant is qualified to serve him.

God is not seeking servants with whom he can share his glory. Rather, God is seeking servants to serve him and **yield** their lives and gifts for his service. He's seeking God-chasers, not glory-seekers.

A **yielded** servant will seek for other **yielded** servants. He will be ever mindful of the price God paid for his sin, spreading that message to all he encounters. He will **yield** his gifts, talents, time, and resources at the feet of God for his use.

I pray that you're seeking to serve him because you love him and want to **yield** your all to his will. It is my hope that you've come to the realization that a life of total surrender is the best gift you can bring to a holy king.

*God, I thank you for pricking our hearts with this word. Lord, you've challenged us with this point, and we are willing to **yield** to you completely. We surrender all we have to you today. Shape us, mold us, and use us for your glory.*

MY SERVANTHOOD NOTES

ZEAL

*Zeal: eagerness and ardent interest in pursuit of
something; fervor; passion*

ZEAL IS THE LAST trait I believe a servant
must possess. **Zeal** speaks of one's excitement
and enthusiasm about something. By now we have
established that ministry is not for everyone. And it's
certainly not for the one who isn't **zealous** about serving
God's people.

There must be something inside of us that makes us
excited when we think about our service to God. There
must be something that keeps us awake at night, anxious
about serving the people of God. I recall the feeling I get
every time I have the opportunity to minister. It's such
an incredible feeling to know that God chose me to serve
his people!

Ministry can easily become a chore for those without
zeal. But to the **zealous** servant, it's a joy, an honor, and
a privilege to serve God and his people. As this book
comes to an end, I pray that you will find joy in serving

God; that you will be **zealous** when serving the people of God, honored that God chose you to serve.

Leaders, consider it an honor to serve the King of kings, and Lord of lords! The Bible admonishes us to let our joy be full! Whenever we serve, let's serve with fullness of joy-- a joy that overflows into all other aspects of your life.

I often say, "You *can't* make a man drink, but you *can* make him thirsty." **Zeal** does just that. Our excitement and **zeal** for something is attractive to others. As we are **zealous**, others will soon begin to inquire as to what it is that makes us so happy. At that point we have just affected and infected them with our **zeal**.

Imagine if everyone within the church had a real **zeal** for God. Imagine if all of our focus and attention was centered on doing the things that make God smile. Then we would not have to compel men to Christ! Instead, they would be running behind us to discover just what it is that has us so enamored with serving God. They'd be asking us why we are so happy and what has us so excited.

There lies a major key for the servant of God-- to have such **zeal** and excitement for God that others want what we have. When we master **zeal**, our lives of service to God will be a blessing to all with whom we come in contact. As we serve with joy and gladness, we will bless the people of God because we're serving God out of a **zealous** heart.

Now comes the time for you to fully commit your life of service to God. You've read each attribute and prayed over each and every one. Now I ask you to make the final commitment. If you're ready--and I pray that you are-- recite this prayer with me now:

Father, I've read each attribute, and I believe that you're calling me to a life of ministry. I feel your gentle tug upon my heart to go deeper into a ministry of service. I cannot do it without you, and I'm relying completely upon you to guide my path. Thank you for this opportunity to look deeper within myself to know your will for my life. I honor you, I bless you, and now I serve you. Amen.

MY SERVANTHOOD NOTES

_____

_____

_____

_____

_____

_____

_____

_____

_____

_____

_____

_____

_____

_____

What Is A Servant?

Written by: Kevin Bond

*A servant is someone who is **able** to lead as well as follow;*
*One who is **bold, confident,** and **dependable.***
*A servant is someone who can **esteem** others as well as*
*himself; **Fearless** in the face of opposition,*
*and **godly** towards all.*
A servant is someone who walks in
humility** and **integrity;
Just** in all his dealings, **kind, loving** and **meek.
*A servant is someone who is **nameless,***
open-minded and patient;
***Quiet** in the face of adversity and*
***resilient** in the face of defeat.*
*A servant is someone who is **stable,***
thoughtful, and unselfish; Valiant,
*but **willing** to fight when necessary.*
*A servant is someone willing to **x-ray** every circumstance;*
*One who is **yielded** to the cause of Christ;*
***Zealous** for the will and purposes of God!*

What Is A Servant? I Am A Servant!

Servant's Prayer

Written by: Kevin Bond © 2003 BMI

CHORUS
O lord I, I will serve you
I will serve you everyday
All my life I, I will praise you
Hear me calling now I pray

I will worship you only
Now I bow before your throne Lord
Holy father hear me calling
This is your servant's prayer Lord

VERSE
When I'm sad you make me happy
Keep me safe from hurt and harm
When I'm burdened or I'm lonely
Comfort me within your arms

Never leave me ever keep me
You I'll follow anywhere Lord
Holy father hear me calling
This is your servant's prayer Lord

BRIDGE

I give to you my life
My all I give to thee
O Lord receive my offering Lord today
This is your servant's prayer

You gave to me your love
Your son at Calvary
O Lord receive my offering Lord today
This is your servant's prayer

Contact Information:

Today, in addition to his production and speaking engagements, Kevin is working as a Worship and Arts Leadership Training Consultant for music departments across the country. So whether your church is in need of organizational structure or is just seeking to be more effective in its operation, rest assured that Kevin Bond is able to help you attain your ministry goals!

For more information contact Kevin Bond at:

678-854-8809 (Office)

775.871.8809 (Fax)

www.KEVINBOND.com (Website)

www.myspace.com/KBONDED (MySpace)